CANADA AT WAR
WORLD WAR II
1939–1945

Weigl

Published by Weigl Educational Publishers Limited
6325 10th Street SE
Calgary, Alberta, Canada
T2H 2Z9

Website: www.weigl.com

Library and Archives Canada Cataloguing in Publication

Baldwin, Douglas, 1944-
        World War II / Douglas Baldwin.
(Canada at War)
Includes index.
Issued also in an electronic format.
ISBN 978-1-55388-720-1 (bound).--ISBN 978-1-55388-724-9 (pbk.)
        1. World War, 1939-1945--Juvenile literature. 2. World War,
1939-1945--Canada--Juvenile literature. 3. Canada--History--
1939-1945--Juvenile literature. I. Title. II. Series: Baldwin, Douglas,
1944- . Canada and her wars.

D743.7.B35 2010   j940.53'71   C2010-903762-6

Printed in the United States of America in North Mankato, Minnesota
1 2 3 4 5 6 7 8 9 0 14 13 12 11 10

072010
WEP230610

Project Coordinator: Heather Kissock
Design: Terry Paulhus
Layout: Kenzie Browne

All of the Internet URLs given in the book were valid at the time of publication. However, due to the dynamic nature
of the Internet, some addresses may have changed, or sites may have ceased to exist since publication. While the
author and publisher regret any inconvenience this may cause readers, no responsibility for any such changes can
be accepted by either the author or the publisher.

Photograph Credits
Cover: Library and Archives Canada; Alamy: pages 10B, 40R, 41R; Corbis: pages 11T, 17B, 34T; CP Images: pages 5T,
5M, 5B, 19B, 24T, 24/25B, 25T, 29T, 33T, 41L, 41M, 43R; Getty Images: pages 4T, 6T, 6M, 6B, 7T, 7B, 8, 9, 10T, 11B, 13,
14B, 15T, 15B, 16, 19TL, 19TR, 21M, 20T, 20BR, 20BL, 21T, 21B, 22, 23, 27, 28, 30T, 31T, 32T, 32/33B, 34B, 35T, 35B,
40L, 42L, 42R; Glenbow Museum: page 12; Library and Archives Canada: pages 4B, 14T, 17TL, 18T, 18B, 26, 29B,
30B, 31B, 43L.

Every reasonable effort has been made to trace ownership and to obtain permission to reprint copyright material.
The publishers would be pleased to have any errors or omissions brought to their attention so that they may be
corrected in subsequent printings.

We acknowledge the financial support of the Government of Canada through the Canada Book Fund for our
publishing activities.

TABLE OF CONTENTS

Canada at War

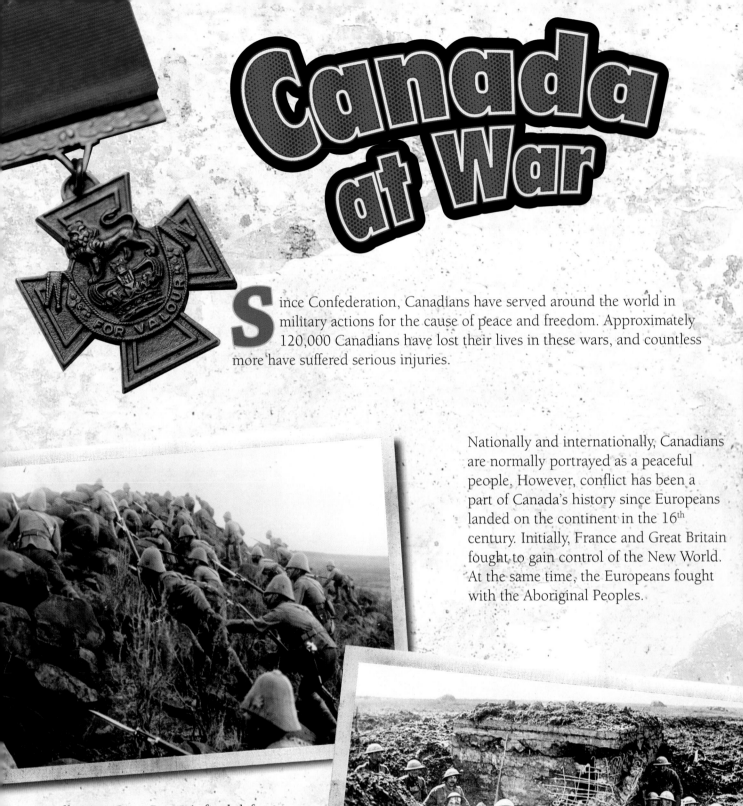

Since Confederation, Canadians have served around the world in military actions for the cause of peace and freedom. Approximately 120,000 Canadians have lost their lives in these wars, and countless more have suffered serious injuries.

Nationally and internationally, Canadians are normally portrayed as a peaceful people, However, conflict has been a part of Canada's history since Europeans landed on the continent in the 16th century. Initially, France and Great Britain fought to gain control of the New World. At the same time, the Europeans fought with the Aboriginal Peoples.

Following Great Britain's final defeat of the French forces in 1759, Canada soon faced a new enemy. In 1775, 1812, 1837, and 1866, the United States attacked Canada. In fact, one of the major reasons for Confederation in 1867 was to create a larger union that could better defend itself from the United States.

After Confederation, Canada remained a British colony and was automatically involved in major conflicts, such as the South African War at the beginning of the 20th century and World War I. It was in this latter war that Canadians earned their reputation as fierce warriors. Although Canada gained true independence in the 1930s, its links to Great Britain remained strong, and Canada entered World War II in 1939 as Great Britain's leading ally.

Since then, Canada has been committed to **multilateralism** and has gone to war only within large multinational coalitions such as in the Korean War, the Gulf War, the war in the Balkans, and the 2001 invasion of Afghanistan. Canada has also played an important role in United Nations peacekeeping operations, committing more troops than many other countries. As of 2006, Canada had the second-highest peacekeeping fatality rate in the world.

Why Another War?

The Treaty of Versailles that ended World War I sowed the seeds for a second world war 20 years later. Germany was angered by the treaty. As part of the treaty, it was forced to sign a statement admitting its guilt for causing the war. The country was also required to pay the costs of the war—ruining Germany's economy. The treaty also forced Germany to cede some of its land to other countries. By dividing the **Austro-Hungarian Empire** into separate countries and creating new countries, such as Poland and Czechoslovakia, the Treaty of Versailles caused frustration and resentment throughout Europe.

As a result of this frustration, **right-wing governments** emerged in several countries. Benito Mussolini assumed power in Italy in 1922, and 11 years later, Adolf Hitler and the Nazi Party gained control of Germany. Hitler blamed Germany's problems on the Treaty of Versailles and on "traitors." To Hitler, traitors consisted of any Jews and Communists living within Germany. Once in power, Hitler began to build Germany's military forces and jailed anyone who spoke out against the Nazi Party. In 1935, the passage of the **Nuremberg Laws** began Hitler's persecution and eventual extermination of German Jews.

▌ As two right-wing European leaders, Mussolini and Hitler met on several occasions in the years leading up to the war and during the war itself.

▌ The Treaty of Versailles was signed on June 28, 1919.

ADOLF HITLER 1889–1945

Adolf Hitler was born in 1889 in an Austrian farming village. At the outbreak of World War I, he joined the German army. Bitter about Germany's defeat, Hitler became active in politics, joining the National Socialist German Workers' Party (Nazi Party) in 1919. He rapidly rose to the top of the party ranks.

Hitler had limited success nationally until the **Great Depression** put many Germans out of work. By 1933, the Nazis were the largest party in the German parliament, and Hitler became **chancellor** of Germany. Within a year and a half, Hitler became the Führer, or the supreme leader of Germany.

In power, Hitler began persecuting those who disagreed with the way he ruled the nation. He also created massive amounts of **propaganda** that strengthened German pride by blaming the country's problems on Communists and Jews. In September 1939, he set out to redraw the map of Europe. His plans led to the outbreak of World War II. When it became clear that Germany was not going to win the war, Adolf Hitler committed suicide in his bunker on April 30, 1945.

At the conclusion of World War I, the Allies, the group of countries that won the war, created the League of Nations to settle international arguments. The League was weakened, however, when the United States refused to join. Sensing the Allies' weakness, in 1936, Germany formed an alliance with Italy and Japan. These countries shared Germany's right-wing political views. Together, these countries became known as the Axis Powers.

Over the next three years, Hitler sought to regain the land that Germany had lost in World War I. Each time Hitler demanded new territory, the Allies gave in. In 1938, Germany seized Austria. Czechoslovakia followed shortly after. When Hitler next demanded the German-speaking areas of Poland, France and Great Britain promised to protect Poland.

▌ In 1921, Hitler created his own private army called the *Sturmabteilung*, or Stormtroopers. The Stormtroopers were known for their willingness to use violence to subdue Hitler's opponents. By the time World War II broke out, Hitler's army had more than two million soldiers.

Sensing rising tension from the Allies, Hitler signed a non-aggression pact with Joseph Stalin of the Soviet Union in August 1939. The two countries agreed not to fight each other for 10 years. This move protected Germany from an eastern attack. With the Soviet Union no longer a potential enemy, Hitler was now ready for war.

On the morning of September 1, 1939, German forces entered Poland. On September 3, Great Britain, France, Australia, and New Zealand declared war on Germany. Canada followed suit a week later. Soon, the world would be consumed by another global war.

▌ Following their invasion of Czechoslovakia in 1939, the German army held a parade on the streets of Prague.

A Global War

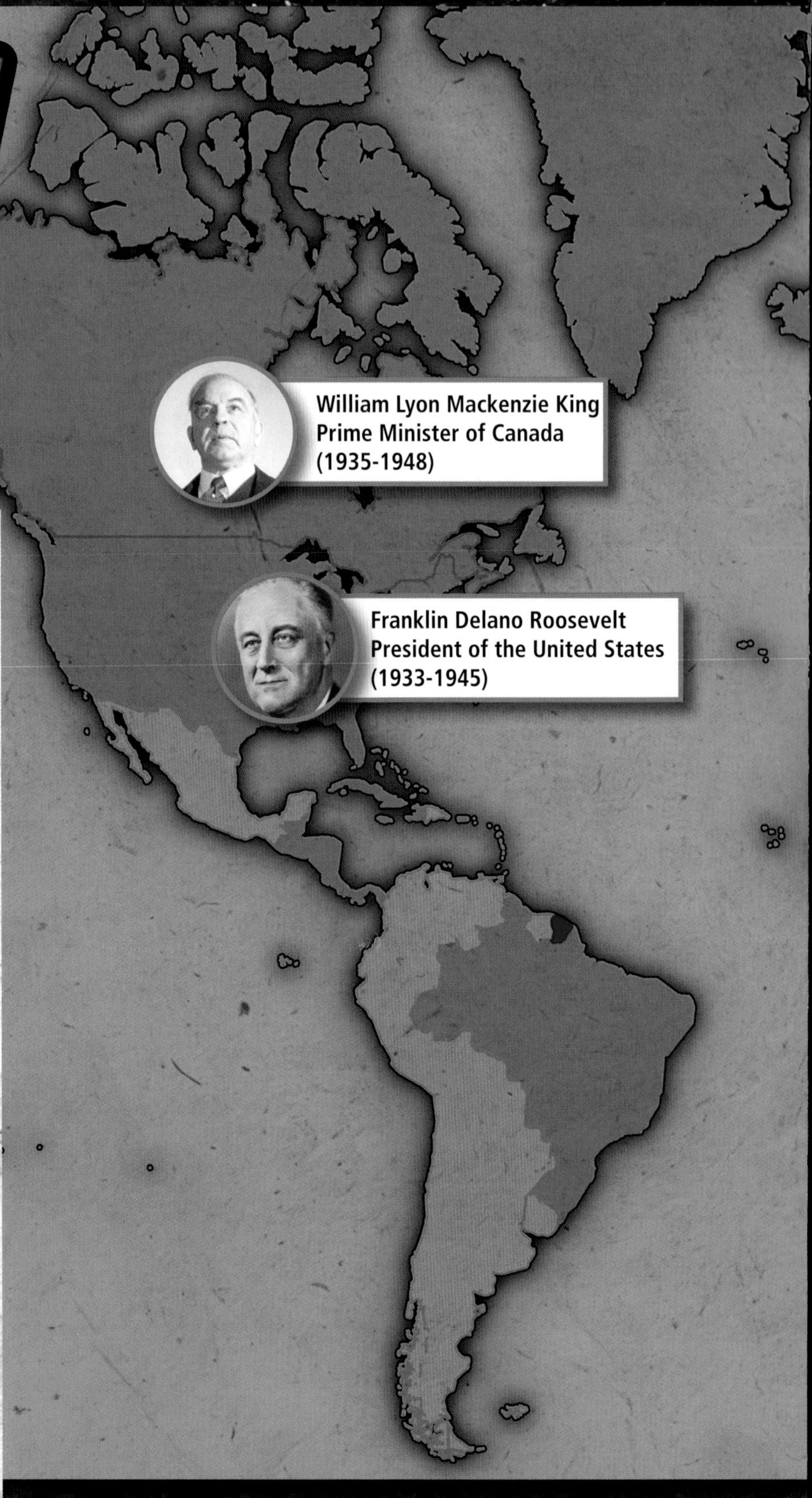

Although World War II started as a European war, it was not long before nations from other parts of the world became involved. Some countries entered the war out of loyalty to former **colonial** ties. Others were forced into the war when they were attacked themselves. Over the course of the war, the **theatres of war** expanded to make this truly a global conflict, with action taking place on land in Europe, Northern Africa, and Asia, and on the waters of both the Atlantic and Pacific Oceans.

The map to the right demonstrates the international scope of World War II and the leaders who played a key role in it.

William Lyon Mackenzie King
Prime Minister of Canada
(1935-1948)

Franklin Delano Roosevelt
President of the United States
(1933-1945)

Allied Powers

Axis Powers and **Occupied** Areas

Neutral

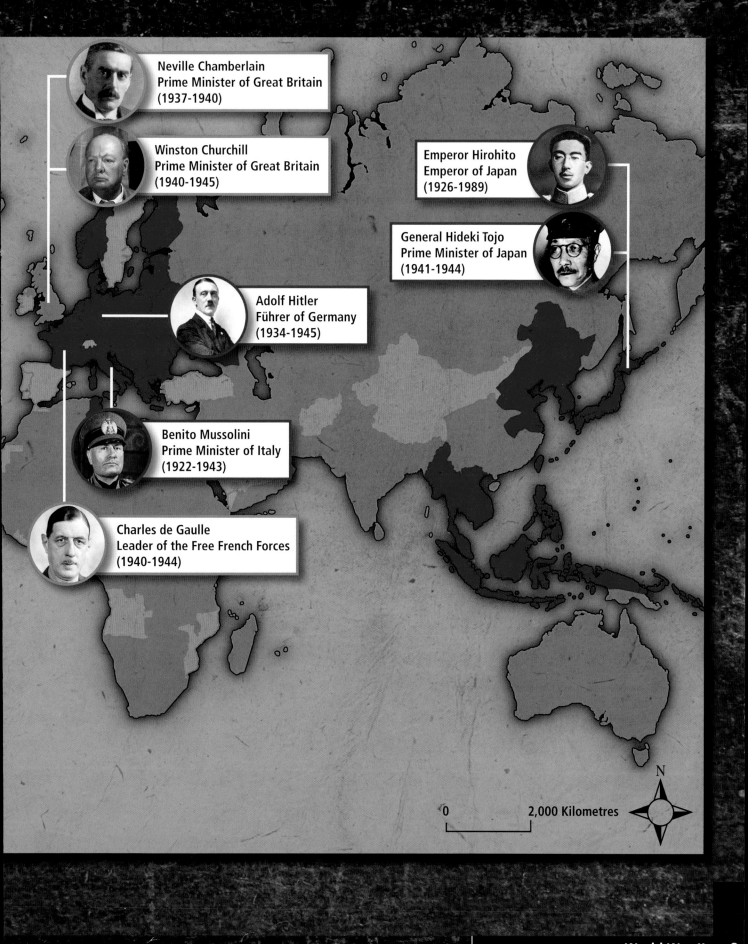

Neville Chamberlain
Prime Minister of Great Britain
(1937-1940)

Winston Churchill
Prime Minister of Great Britain
(1940-1945)

Emperor Hirohito
Emperor of Japan
(1926-1989)

General Hideki Tojo
Prime Minister of Japan
(1941-1944)

Adolf Hitler
Führer of Germany
(1934-1945)

Benito Mussolini
Prime Minister of Italy
(1922-1943)

Charles de Gaulle
Leader of the Free French Forces
(1940-1944)

0   2,000 Kilometres

N

Canada Declares War

anadian Prime Minister William Lyon Mackenzie King had done everything he could to prevent another world war. At the **Imperial Conference of 1937**, King had urged Great Britain to give in to Hitler's demands, rather than go to war. When British Prime Minister Neville Chamberlain later agreed to let Hitler have part of Czechoslovakia, King sent him a telegram of appreciation.

When France and Great Britain declared war against Germany on September 3, King was still in favour of appeasing Hitler. King remembered how World War I and the issue of **conscription** had divided Canada. He wanted to avoid another world war at all costs.

For this reason, Canada remained neutral for the week after Great Britain declared war. King wanted to put the issue of going to war to a vote before the House of Commons. However, within that week, the Germans torpedoed an unarmed passenger ship, killing four Canadians on board. When it came time for the House of Commons to vote, only one member of Parliament voted against going to war. As a result, Canada declared war as an independent country for the first time.

▌ Neville Chamberlain resigned from his position as prime minister of Great Britain in 1940. He was succeeded by Winston Churchill.

▌ The unarmed passenger ship SS *Athenia* was torpedoed on Great Britain's first day at war. Besides the four Canadians killed, another 113 people lost their lives. Many more were injured.

Although Canadians were united in their desire to stop Hitler, Canada was not prepared for war. King had deliberately allowed the armed forces to decline in numbers and weaponry during the Great Depression. The navy consisted of just 1,800 soldiers and 15 ships. The army had only about 4,300 soldiers, and the air force approximately 4,100 soldiers. Equipment for both the air force and army was minimal and dated to the point of being obsolete.

Still, when Canada declared war, thousands of people lined up at recruitment centres to enlist. The government then began implementing its own plans to prepare Canada for war, developing training programs for enlistees and producing the equipment and munitions needed to fight.

▌ Shortly after Canada declared war, soldiers from across the country began boarding ships bound for Europe.

▌ On September 10, 1939, Parliament convened to hear Lord Tweedsmuir, the country's governor general, read Canada's declaration of war.

Canadians Who Served In World War II

Canadians figured prominently in World War II. The Royal Canadian Navy organized supply **convoys** to provide Great Britain with food and other goods. Canadian pilots helped stop Hitler in the **Battle of Britain** and other air battles. Canadian soldiers fought bravely on the battlefields of Europe and Asia and played an important role in the **D-Day** invasion of Western Europe.

Over the course of the war, 1.1 million Canadians served in the armed forces. More than 45,000 lost their lives.

The British Commonwealth Air Training Plan

Shortly after Canada entered the war, Prime Minister Mackenzie King offered to train pilots as Canada's major contribution to the war effort. The program under which this training took place became known as the British Commonwealth Air Training Plan (BCATP). When King made this commitment, the Royal Canadian Air Force (RCAF) had only about 4,100 personnel and fewer than a dozen airports. The RCAF had to recruit instructors, build air bases, acquire aircraft, and develop training schools. By the time the program ended, Canada had established 151 training schools across the country.

Most of the instructors and staff at the schools were Canadian, but the recruits came from all over the world. Once they arrived at their training facility, they trained under a strict regimen. They had to complete their courses quickly to keep the air war on track. Total training took 38 to 45 weeks. The pilots were then considered ready for war and were sent overseas. Besides training potential pilots, the program also provided instruction for navigators, wireless radio operators, air gunners, air bombers, and flight engineers.

By the end of the war, the BCATP had graduated 131,533 pilots, observers, flight engineers, and other aircrew for the air forces of Canada, West Indies, Great Britain, Australia, New Zealand, France, Czechoslovakia, Norway, and Poland.

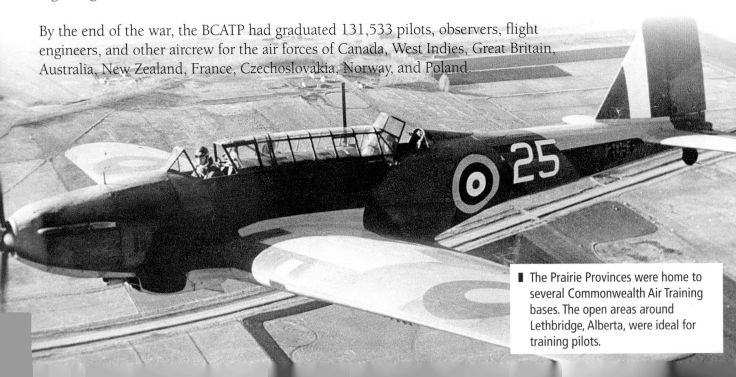

❚ The Prairie Provinces were home to several Commonwealth Air Training bases. The open areas around Lethbridge, Alberta, were ideal for training pilots.

Canadians in the Battle of the Atlantic

At the outbreak of the war, Canada's navy consisted of 1,800 soldiers and 15 warships. By the end of the war, the Royal Canadian Navy (RCN) had nearly 100,000 sailors and 365 ships. It was the third-largest navy in the world.

Much of the navy's growth can be attributed to the Battle of the Atlantic, which was an effort on Hitler's part to prevent Great Britain from receiving needed food and war materials from North America. German u-boats, or submarines, searched the waters of the Atlantic Ocean to find merchant ships carrying essential goods to Great Britain. The u-boats were ordered to destroy any ships that they found. In effect, the Battle of the Atlantic was a battle for Great Britain's very survival.

When Germany pushed its submarine attacks farther into the North Atlantic in 1941, St. John's, Newfoundland, became the home of the Newfoundland Escort Force (NEF). Made up of ships from the Royal Canadian Navy, the United States Navy, and Great Britain's Royal Navy, the NEF's job was to escort convoys of ships from North America to Ireland. The RCN played a major role in these convoys, contributing six destroyers and 17 **corvettes** to the force.

The NEF's job was to find and sink u-boats before they could attack the merchant ships. The RCAF flew anti-submarine missions and gave air cover to the vessels while warships escorted the convoys across the ocean. The Battle of the Atlantic lasted six years, and was a hard-fought battle for sea supremacy. Ultimately, the Allied forces won this battle.

❚ More than 1,000 German u-boats were used in the Battle of the Atlantic. They were responsible for the sinking of almost 3,000 Allied ships.

THE WOMEN'S DIVISIONS

In World War I, the only women allowed in Canada's armed forces were nurses. This situation changed in World War II. The creation of the Canadian Women's Army Corps (CWAC) in 1941 happened for two reasons. The government knew that, over time, the army would need more workers. As well, Canadian women were vocal in their desire to join the armed forces. They exerted pressure on the federal government to change the requirements in favour of women.

Once the CWAC was approved, criteria were established to determine who could enlist. These standards were to be strictly enforced. Recruits had to be British subjects, single, and between the ages of 18 and 45. They could have no dependents. In terms of education, they had to have completed, at minimum, grade eight. Physically, all recruits had to weigh at least 47.6 kilograms, and be at least 160 centimetres tall. They had to be in excellent health. Once enlisted, recruits were given basic fitness training to develop strength and discipline.

▮ Members of the Canadian Women's Army Corps were sent overseas to serve in countries such as Italy.

Soon after the CWAC was established, other arms of the forces also created women's corps. The Canadian Women's Auxiliary Air Force was created in December 1941. The Women's Royal Canadian Naval Service followed in July 1942.

Eventually, Canada had 45,000 servicewomen, many of whom were posted overseas. These women served in a wide variety of non-combat roles, such as radar operators, truck and ambulance drivers, parachute riggers, nurses, secretaries, and mechanics. Some of these women often found themselves in the heat of battle. They were bombed, shelled, and torpedoed. Others were made prisoners of war. More than 240 women won medals for bravery. In total, 73 were killed, and many others were wounded. All of the women made a significant contribution to the war effort and paved the way to the integration of women in Canadian armed forces.

▮ Some Canadian women served as members of the Air Transport Auxiliary in England. This unit transferred new, repaired, or damaged airplanes between factories.

CAMP X

Intelligence was an important part of World War II. Whether breaking enemy codes or working undercover behind enemy lines, intelligence agents gathered valuable information about Germany and the Axis Powers. Many of the Allied intelligence agents, or spies, were trained at Camp X, which was erected on the shores of Lake Ontario near Oshawa, Ontario. Candidates selected to train at Camp X included the members of the Federal Bureau of Investigation (FBI), the Royal Canadian Mounted Police (RCMP), U.S. Army Intelligence, and U.S. Naval Intelligence.

The camp's curriculum covered a variety of intelligence and **infiltration** techniques. The camp taught agents how to use firearms, parachute, read maps, gain access to enemy areas, use explosives, disguise themselves, and employ psychological warfare. Physical training included hand-to-hand combat techniques, and strength and endurance exercises. Agents were also trained how to recruit agents and how to use propaganda effectively.

The camp operated from 1941 to 1944. During that time, hundreds of agents graduated from the training program. Many of these spy school graduates were Canadians who went on to serve in places such as France, Yugoslavia, Hungary, Italy, Burma, and Malaysia. As part of their work, agents organized resistance and sabotage within occupied countries, helped prisoners of war escape, and helped downed Allied airmen evade enemy capture in **occupied** Europe.

▮ Ian Fleming, the creator of James Bond spy novels, is believed to have trained at Camp X.

▮ Spying was a dangerous job. If caught, spies sometimes faced immediate execution.

Heroic Canadians

The men and women who enlisted for World War II came from a range of backgrounds. What united them was a desire to fight for their country. While all performed heroic acts, as the war progressed, some names became more known than others. Some soldiers were hailed for their brilliant war strategies and strong leadership. Others were celebrated because they performed feats unlike anyone else in the war.

WILLIAM STEPHENSON
(1896–1989)

"Nothing deceives like a document."

William Stephenson was born in Winnipeg, Manitoba, in 1896. While a student at the University of Manitoba, he invented a system that allowed for the wireless transmission of pictures from one place to another. His career as an inventor was interrupted, however, when World War I began. Stephenson enlisted and became a fighter pilot, surviving two gas attacks and recording 26 "kills" as a pilot. Following the war, he moved to Great Britain, where he made a fortune selling his invention to newspapers. His success allowed him to rise through the ranks of British society and make important connections in the British government.

When World War II began, Stephenson was put in charge of British Security Co-ordination in the Western Hemisphere. He moved to New York to assume the position. There, he led an army of code-breakers, spies, assassins, and sabotage experts. He also was instrumental in the creation of Camp X.

For his efforts in the behind-the-scenes aspect of the war, he was knighted by King George VI of Great Britain. He was also awarded the Order of Canada in 1979.

After World War II ended, Stephenson moved to the Caribbean. He died in Bermuda in 1989 at the age of 92.

TOMMY PRINCE
(1915—1977)

Aboriginal Peoples fought in every major battle and campaign of the war. More than 3,000 **status** Aboriginals, as well as an unknown number of Inuit and Métis, enlisted. At least 17 were **decorated** for bravery in action. One such person was Tommy Prince.

Thomas George Prince was born on October 25, 1915, in Manitoba. He was raised on the Brokenhead Reserve. He joined the army in 1940 and gradually became a member of the Devil's Brigade, a special assault team. Prince became known for his bravery on the field. He once stepped in front of German troops to repair a damaged communications wire. Another time, he walked deep behind enemy lines to find an enemy camp. At the end of the war, he was awarded two medals for his bravery.

When Canada became involved in the Korean War, Prince enlisted and was again awarded medals for his efforts. As a result, Prince became the most decorated Aboriginal soldier in Canada's armed forces.

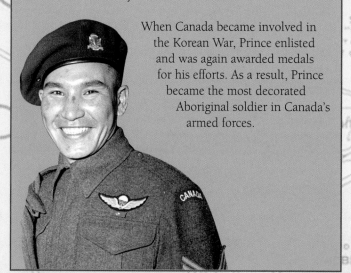

MONA PARSONS
(1901—1976)

Nova Scotia-born Mona Parsons was the only Canadian woman captured by Nazis, tried, and sent to a prison camp.

Until the war, Parsons had lived a privileged life. The daughter of a successful businessman, she trained as an actress, eventually moving to New York City. When her acting career stalled, she turned to a career in nursing. In 1937, she married a Dutch millionaire, Willem Leonhardt, and moved to Holland.

When the war began, the couple joined a **resistance group** that aided fallen airmen. In 1941, they were betrayed by a Nazi informant and arrested. Initially, Parsons was sentenced to death by firing squad. She appealed that decision, and her sentence was changed to life in prison.

In 1945, Parsons escaped and made her way to the Allied lines. Eventually, she reached a Canadian **battalion**.

Parsons and her husband were reunited after the war. When he died in 1956, she returned to Nova Scotia. She died there in 1976.

GEORGE "BUZZ" BEURLING
(1921—1948)

George Beurling was born in Quebec in 1921. As a boy, airplanes and flying fascinated him. When World War II broke out, he enlisted with the Royal Air Force (RAF) as a pilot. There, he earned the nickname "Buzz" for his risk-taking flying techniques. He liked to fly low over the ground, and would often separate himself from his flying formation to attack enemy planes.

Taking risks made Buzz Canada's top-scoring pilot of World War II. While serving with the RAF in Malta, Buzz shot down 29 enemy planes. Of them, 27 were brought down over a period of only four months. After Buzz transferred to the Royal Canadian Air Force in 1943, he shot down three more enemy planes, bringing his total to 31. His wartime exploits were rewarded with the Distinguished Flying Medal, the Distinguished Flying Cross, and the Distinguished Service Medal.

Following the war, Buzz agreed to fly planes for the Israeli army. However, en route to Israel from Rome, his plane caught on fire and crashed, killing Buzz and another pilot.

Technology in the War

Soldiers had a variety of equipment and weaponry at their disposal during World War II. Many of these tools had been used in prior wars, but advancements in technology brought battles in the air, at sea, and on the ground to a new level. Canada played an important role in manufacturing some of this equipment.

SHIPS OF WAR

Starting in 1940, Canadian shipyards increased their production tenfold in order to provide the RCN with destroyers, corvettes, frigates, and minesweepers.

Each type of ship created had a specific purpose. Destroyers were fast ships designed for anti-torpedo and anti-submarine warfare. Corvettes were smaller vessels used to patrol the coast and escort other vessels. Frigates were faster, more comfortable, and better armed than corvettes. They were used to escort convoys and for anti-submarine warfare.

Minesweepers were used to dislodge mines the Germans placed in the water. These ships dragged steel wire through the water to dislodge the mines. When they came to the surface, the mines were destroyed with rifle fire.

Landing craft were small ships specially designed to carry troops and weapons in preparation for an amphibious assault.

GUNS

As the war progressed, both Allied and Axis forces employed ever-more sophisticated technology to create efficient killing machines. The basic **infantry** weapons were the Lee-Enfield rifle and Bren light machine-gun. They were supplemented by **artillery** such as mortars and howitzers. This equipment could fire ammunition at a steep angle so that it flew over the enemy and dropped directly down on them. Some soldiers also used semi-automatic rifles such as the Sten gun.

TANKS

One of the most common tanks used in World War II was the Valentine. Many of these tanks were manufactured in Canada, at a plant in Montreal. Since they were slow, had thin armour and limited firepower, the Valentines were eventually replaced by the Canadian-built Ram tank. By 1943, however, American Sherman tanks were common. For water use, the Sherman was fitted with a collapsible canvas screen, which inflated around the hull of the tank, allowing it to float. Two propellers were fitted at the rear of the tank.

MINES

The British and Canadian navies used three types of floating mines. These were the magnetic, the acoustic, and the contact mines. Each mine detonated in different ways. The contact mine exploded when it came in touch with the hull of a vessel, whereas the sound of a ship's propeller detonated the acoustic mine. The magnetic field emitted by a ship's hull activated the magnetic mine. Both Allied and Axis forces used floating mines that were moored to the bottom of the ocean, particularly in the English Channel.

AERIAL WARFARE

Great strides were made in aircraft technology between World War I and II. The aircraft used in World War II had more capabilities, including the ability to travel farther and carry more weight. As a result, aerial warfare played a major role in World War II.

The key strategy used by both Allied and Axis forces was the bombing raid, in which bomber planes flew over targets en masse. The goal of these constant raids was to break down the enemy's defences, economy, and morale. Initially, the British forces favoured precision bombing, in which specific targets were attacked. These targets included factories, oil refineries, and naval yards. When this did not achieve the required results, the British turned to area bombing, in which entire cities were bombed.

Several types of bombers were used throughout the war. All had to cross Germany's daunting anti-aircraft defence lines in order to reach their targets. The Vickers Wellington was a medium-sized, twin-engine bomber that could carry 1,315 kilograms of bombs. It was often used in night bombings. Over time, however, it was replaced with larger, four-engine bombers, such as the Avro Lancaster. The Avro Lancaster had a longer range than the Vickers Wellington and could carry up to up to 6,350 kilograms of bombs. Besides bombing raids, this aircraft was also used to drop food to countries under siege.

The Science of World War II

The war was a battle of scientific minds as much as it was of bullets and bombs. Much of the research conducted to win the war found **civilian** uses afterwards and helped shape today's world. Canadians played a role in the development of several inventions and scientific breakthroughs during World War II.

ENIGMA

Germany communicated with its submarines and air force using an **encrypted** system called Enigma. A machine similar to a typewriter produced coded messages that could only be read by someone who had a similar machine. The machines used a system of rotors and electrical currents to create messages. The combinations under which the rotors and currents worked was constantly changed so that the enemy could not decipher the messages being sent. British intelligence created a team of cryptography experts to break the code. Using information provided by Polish code breakers, they were able to break the coding system in 1940. Breaking the Enigma code ultimately won the Battle of the Atlantic as it allowed Allied forces to track German u-boats.

RADAR

RADAR (Radio Detection and Ranging) was developed in the 1930s and was put to good use in World War II to locate German u-boats, ships, and aircraft. The RADAR system is made up of a transmitter and receiver. The transmitter emits radio waves over a broad area. When the waves encounter a solid object, they are reflected back to the receiver. The receiver converts the waves into a signal that a RADAR operator can see. Due to the speed at which the signal travels, the RADAR operator can estimate the object's direction and distance.

The military used RADAR in two ways. First, it was used to scan large areas for purposes of mapping and navigation. This allowed the military to monitor enemy activity to determine the level of threat. As well, ground forces could use RADAR to direct the air force to incoming enemy aircraft.

RADAR was also used for more precision work. Once incoming aircraft or ships were detected, RADAR onboard allied planes and ships allowed the operators to locate an exact target and fire upon it. This was especially useful in night fighting, when operators could not see the target on their own.

DEGAUSSING

Naval forces played an integral role in World War II, but they were often placed in the most vulnerable of situations. Not only did they have to deal with u-boats lurking in the waters below them, they also had to deal with the fact that the metal that their ships were made of attracted mines. To protect the ships and the soldiers on board, scientists worked to find a way to demagnetize the ships so that mines would not be drawn to them. A key researcher in this area was Charles Goodeve, from Neepawa, Manitoba.

Goodeve came up with the process of degaussing to reduce the magnetic field of the ship. Also called wiping, the results were achieved by running a electrical cable up and down the ship's hull. The electricity interacted with the metal to neutralize the ship's magnetic field, thus minimizing the threat of magnetic mines.

THE TIME IS NEAR

Projectiles, such as bullets and torpedoes, were common weapons of war prior to World War II. However, they were limited by their mode of operation. Projectiles either exploded upon impact with their targets, or they exploded when their timer went off. Accuracy in aiming or in timing was essential for the projectile to achieve its goals. This became difficult in World War II due to advances in technology. Machinery could move faster than ever before. The needed accuracy was difficult to achieve.

The British government began experimenting with the idea of a projectile that could sense its proximity to a target and detonate on its own. Eventually, a laboratory in the United States developed a proximity fuze to be placed inside explosive devices.

The proximity fuze relied on electronics to gauge proximity to a target. The fuze consisted of a radio transmitter and receiver. The transmitter would send out a constant signal, which would reflect off the target, sending it to the receiver. The frequency of the signal would increase as the projectile moved closer to its target. When the signal reached a specific intensity, the requisite proximity was reached, and the explosive detonated. Other types of fuzes were also developed, which relied on different types of sensing equipment, including lenses and **photo cells**, magnetic fields, and microphones.

One problem with the design of the fuze was that it had the potential to initiate detonation too early. When the projectile was fired, there was always the possibility that the fuze would sense the ship or airplane it was being sent from and detonate immediately. To fix this problem, a Canadian by the name of George Klein developed a timing device that made it possible to safely deploy the projectile.

ANTI-SUBMARINE PROTECTION

Until 1943, German u-boats could close in on convoys, fire torpedoes, and move on without being detected. Allied scientists developed the anti-submarine detection system (ASDIC) to counteract the u-boat menace. This underwater detection, or sonar, system emits a sound signal at regular intervals. The sound waves emitted from the ASDIC system travel through water and, when they hit a solid body, bounce back as an echo. The position of the u-boat is estimated based on the direction of the echo. Its distance is based on the delay between emission and interception.

NUCLEAR RESEARCH

As the war went on, scientists on both sides of the conflict worked to develop weapons and technologies that would give them the edge. Nuclear weaponry grew from this research. Nuclear weapons rely on specific elements, such as plutonium, uranium, or hydrogen, to create **fission** or **fusion** reactions, which in turn produce explosions.

In order to learn more about the physics of the fission process and the role **heavy water** played in it, Canada built a nuclear reactor in Ontario. Called the Zero Energy Experimental Pile (ZEEP), it was the first nuclear reactor to be built outside of the United States. One of the key engineers involved in the project was George Klein.

ZEEP produced its first nuclear reaction on September 5, 1945. From that point, it was used to research the fission process. The knowledge acquired from ZEEP experiments led to the creation of Canada's CANDU reactor, one of the best-known nuclear power reactors in the world.

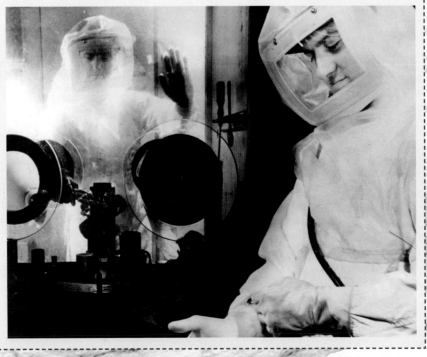

I n the early years of the war, Canada was Great Britain's only close ally. Canadian pilots fought bravely in the Battle of the Atlantic. They tasted bitter defeats in Hong Kong and at Dieppe and gained costly victories participating in the D-Day invasion of Europe. Canadians later earned the enduring respect and affection of the people and countries they rescued from Hitler's armies in northern Europe.

The Fall of Hong Kong, 1941

The first Canadian military engagement of the war took place in the British colony of Hong Kong. In autumn 1941, most people did not expect a Japanese attack. Nearly 2,000 Canadian troops from the Royal Rifles of Canada and the Winnipeg Grenadiers were stationed on **garrison duty** in Hong Kong. Most of them had little military training and many had never fired their rifles or thrown a grenade.

Beginning on December 7, 1941, Japan launched surprise attacks on the U.S. naval bases at Pearl Harbor in Hawaii, Northern Malaya, the Philippines, Guam, Wake Island, and Hong Kong. At 8 a.m. on December 8, Japanese aircraft either destroyed or damaged all RAF aircraft in Hong Kong. This stirred the British forces on the island, which had about 14,000 British, Canadian, and Indian soldiers in total, to action.

▌ The United States had stayed neutral in the war until the bombing of Pearl Harbor. After losing more than 2,300 American citizens, 188 airplanes, and their entire Pacific fleet of warships in the space of three hours, the United States saw no other choice but to fight in the war.

To reduce the British force's ability to fight back, Japan bombed the island with artillery fire and air raids. Even so, Hong Kong repeatedly refused to surrender. However, with no help on the way following Pearl Harbor, the fall of the colony was only a matter of time.

The final Japanese invasion of Hong Kong came at nightfall on December 18. It was supported by heavy artillery fire, total air control, and the knowledge that Japanese reinforcements were quickly available. The Allies were exhausted from the nonstop bombardment and days of continuous action. The Canadians held out until their ammunition, food, and water were depleted, but, after almost 18 full days of fighting, the defence of Hong Kong was over.

The remaining Allied soldiers were captured and spent the rest of the war in Japanese prison camps. Of the 1,975 Canadian soldiers who went to Hong Kong, 290 died in battle, and 267 died in the brutal Japanese prisoner of war camps. One-half of the Canadians who went to Hong Kong were either killed or wounded. This was one of the highest casualty rates for a Canadian theatre of action during all of World War II.

"I cannot bring myself to write what happened between the 18th and the 25th. All I can say is that I saw too many brave men die, some were my best friends and died beside me."

-Thomas Forsyth, Winnipeg Grenadiers, *"War Diary & Memoirs,"* Library and Archives Canada, Recorded after the fighting finished on December 25, 1941

▌ Following the Battle of Hong Kong, all remaining members of the British forces were shipped to Japanese prisoner of war camps.

The Dieppe Raid, 1942

On the morning of August 19, 1942, nearly 5,000 Canadian soldiers, 1,000 British soldiers, and 65 American and French soldiers crouched in landing crafts off the heavily fortified French port of Dieppe. They were supported by four destroyers and 74 Allied air squadrons, including eight from the RCAF. The plan was to seize Dieppe, destroy the port and airport, take prisoners, and return to England. The key to victory was in the surprise of the attack.

However, some of the Allied ships had gone off course and arrived late, so the raid did not start until broad daylight. As well, the Germans had spotted the enemy ships during the night. The element of surprise was lost. When the first Canadians hit the beach, the Germans were waiting.

The Germans had fortified the towering cliffs around the beach with **pillboxes**, howitzers, and mortars. All were aimed at the oncoming Allied soldiers. Allied air strikes had been scheduled to eliminate these fortifications before the troops hit land, but they were cancelled, and the fortifications remained active. Many landing craft were blown out of the water before troops made it to shore. Most of the soldiers who made it to the beach were cut down by German machine gun fire.

■ Medical corps did their best to evacuate wounded soldiers from the Dieppe beach. However, the evacuation had to be cut short due to the fighting that was still taking place. As a result, more than 3,300 soldiers, including approximately 2,000 Canadians, were left behind to die or be taken prisoner.

Evacuating the area of Allied forces was impossible in the face of German fire. The Allied forces suffered major losses as a result. One Canadian regiment had 96 percent casualties. The Royal Air Force lost 106 aircraft—more than in any other day of the war. The RCAF lost 13 planes.

Of the 4,963 Canadians who embarked for Dieppe, only 2,210 returned to England, and many of them were seriously wounded. The lessons learned at Dieppe helped the Allies in subsequent battles, but at an enormous cost.

▌ Tanks that were scheduled to support infantry troops were late arriving. The infantry had to start fighting without artillery backup.

The Battle of Juno Beach, 1944

The invasion of northwest Europe began on June 6, 1944, with Allied landings on the coast of Normandy. This was D-Day, the day that began the liberation of Europe. It was part of a larger operation called Operation Overlord.

Following an all-night air bombardment, the Allies attacked on land. Just before dawn, **paratroopers** dropped behind enemy lines. In the early morning, 14,000 Canadian troops and 4,000 British troops landed on a stretch of beach code-named "Juno."

All three Canadian services shared in the assault. Royal Canadian Navy minesweepers cleared lanes through the English Channel. Canadian naval guns hammered enemy beaches. The RCN's assault landing craft carried Canadian soldiers to shore. The Royal Canadian Air Force attacked German **batteries**, and the Canadian Parachute Battalion dropped down to help protect the landing area.

The Queen's Own Rifles was the first Canadian regiment to land. They ran a 200-metre dash to the cover of a seawall. There, they faced guns that had not been seen on previous **reconnaissance missions**. These guns wiped out almost an entire **platoon** before they were destroyed.

■ The waters had been choppy on the trip to Juno Beach. Many soldiers were still feeling the effects of seasickness when they headed into the barrage of enemy fire.

The Canadian soldiers' orders were to destroy enemy resistance on the beach and push their way 12 kilometres to the town of Caen and the Carpiquet airfield. The task was formidable because the Germans had turned the coastline into a continuous fortress, with guns, pillboxes, barbed wire, mines, and beach obstacles. The Canadians had to fight hard every step of the way, but they finally reached Caen on July 9.

Approximately 4,500 Allied soldiers lost their lives on D-Day. By the end of Operation Overlord, Allied deaths totalled more than 53,000. Two nearby cemeteries contain the bodies of nearly 5,000 Canadians killed during Operation Overlord. Another 13,000 Canadians were wounded.

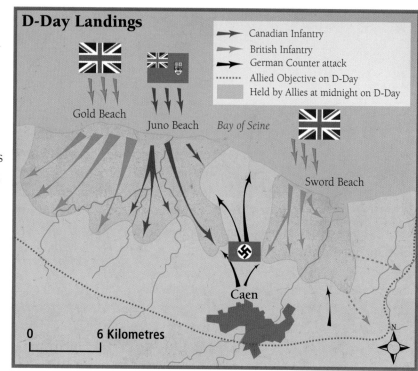

D-Day Landings

→ Canadian Infantry
→ British Infantry
→ German Counter attack
⋯ Allied Objective on D-Day
▢ Held by Allies at midnight on D-Day

Gold Beach
Juno Beach
Bay of Seine
Sword Beach
Caen

0   6 Kilometres

N

> "Those last few moments were awful, it was the waiting that was hard. We were coming under pretty intense small arms fire by this time. At last the gangways were run down, and it was a case of get up and get in and get down. I manoeuvred into position to be as near as possible to the front. I wanted to be one of the first to land, not because of any heroics, but waiting your turn on the exposed ramp was much worse than going in."
>
> *Unknown Canadian soldier,
> Warren Tute Collection,
> D-Day Museum*

The Home Front

The war affected almost every aspect of day-to-day life in Canada. Towns and cities bustled with activity as factories converted to round-the-clock production of military equipment. Military planes could often be seen flying overhead, performing training exercises. Soldiers on leave returned home to visit familiar haunts. Beginning in January 1942, the threat of invasion from the skies led to a series of blackouts and air raid drills that made everyone aware of the dangers of war.

The war was also prevalent in the media. Radio stations, cinemas, newspapers, and magazines featured constant news updates, and advertisements from the government and citizens groups promoted the war effort. Even comic books had military themes.

Growing Up in War

Children and teenagers played an important role in the war effort. Many Canadian soldiers were teenagers when they enlisted to fight. About 700,000 Canadians under the age of 21 served in the war. Boys as young as 13 lied about their age and enlisted.

Canadian children were encouraged by their family and community to support the war. Some worked on farms to help maintain a steady food supply for Canada and its Allies. Many schools did not count attendance or introduce new material in classes until after the crops were harvested. The minimum age for acquiring a driver's licence was lowered to 14 so that farm children could legally operate farm equipment.

Some students made socks and scarves for soldiers at lunch hour. They wrote letters to prisoners of war. Encouraged by such incentives as free passes to movies, children donated their toys for metal salvage drives. The metal was melted down and used to create equipment for the war. Many children planted victory gardens at home or in school baseball diamonds. These were gardens planted to relieve food shortages.

■ Victory gardens were not unique to Canada. They were promoted in several countries, including Great Britain and the United States.

Women in a War Society

During World War II, the role of women in Canadian society changed dramatically. Many women assumed the jobs that had once been filled by men who were now at war. Most of these jobs were in factories, where they turned raw materials into tanks, planes, and ships.

In rural Canada, women took over farming jobs vacated by men who went overseas. One Alberta mother of nine sons—all of whom were either in the army or working in factories—took on all the work they had once done. This included ploughing the fields, tending to the farm animals, and hauling grain to elevators. All the while, she continued to do her work as well by looking after her garden and canning fruits and vegetables for winter use.

Women also helped recycle and collect materials needed for the war effort. They knit socks, scarves, and mitts and prepared parcels for Canadians overseas. They made their own clothes and planted victory gardens to supply much-needed fruits and vegetables to their families and communities. Many women joined volunteer clubs to improve the morale of the troops overseas. These clubs packaged canvas "ditty bags" with items such as chocolates, sewing kits, and razor blades to send to soldiers.

▌ Canadian women played an important role in the construction of military airplanes, including the *Hawker Hurricane*.

THE ECONOMY

The need for equipment and ammunition brought an end to the economic hardship of the Great Depression. Instead, Canada was faced with the challenge of creating a strong industrial base to produce weapons and war materials. By 1941, there were enough jobs for all who wanted them.

World War II was highly mechanized, with a great deal of mass-production of weapons, ammunition, vehicles, and other war materials. Over the course of the war, Canadian industries produced military equipment of all kinds, including more than 800,000 military transport vehicles, 50,000 tanks, 40,000 field, naval, and anti-aircraft guns, and 1,700,000 small arms.

Government Intervention

The massive effort needed to win the war forced the government to become actively involved in almost every sector of society. It planned daycare programs for working mothers and enforced wage and pricing controls. Government involvement also extended into the personal lives of Canadians, affecting communication between soldiers and their families.

Determined to stop any news or talk that would damage the Allied cause, the government censored information it felt could jeopardize the war effort. This included information about the locations of troops and training exercises. All mail from Canadian families to prisoners of war overseas was censored for information that might be passed on to the enemy. The government also monitored war information in newspapers, radio, and film.

▮ During the war, it was common for people to receive mail that had already been opened and read by government officials.

Japanese Internment

The Canadian government was deeply suspicious of ethnic groups whose homelands were at war with Canada. German and Italian Canadians were forced to register with the police so their activities could be tracked. Some were arrested as a threat against the country. Japanese Canadians, however, suffered a worse fate.

Japanese aggression in Asia, the attack on Pearl Harbor, and the fall of Hong Kong caused many Canadians to fear that British Columbia might be attacked next. Anti-Japanese feelings grew to extreme levels in British Columbia. Early in 1942, the federal government confiscated all Japanese-owned fishing boats, motor vehicles, cameras, and radios. The government also ordered the **internment** of approximately 750 Japanese men who had been judged to be security risks. All persons of Japanese descent were evacuated from the coastal areas of British Columbia. More than 21,000 Japanese, 75 percent of whom were Canadian-born, were forced to leave their homes and their jobs on 24 hours notice and were sent to camps that had been set up across the country.

At the end of the war, the federal government tried to force people of Japanese descent to leave British Columbia and move to eastern Canada or settle in Japan. Approximately 4,000 of them took the second alternative because they could see no future for themselves in Canada.

▮ The evacuation of Japanese Canadians from the West Coast was one of the greatest mass movements of people in Canadian history.

Mackenzie King and Conscription

When the war began, national unity was Prime Minister Mackenzie King's most important goal. King wanted to avoid the turmoil that the issue of conscription had caused in World War I. When Canada entered the war on September 10, 1939, King promised that there would be no conscription. However, as the war progressed and more soldiers were needed, the majority of Canadians supported King's decision in June 1940 to conscript young men to serve only for home defence duties. Canadians who served overseas volunteered for such duties.

To King's dismay, in 1941 many English Canadians began to push for overseas conscription. King stalled. Japan's entry into the war in December 1941, however, brought further calls for overseas conscription. Finally, he held a national **referendum**. King asked Canadians if they would release him from his promise not to impose conscription for overseas service. Quebec voted 73 percent "no." The rest of the country voted 64 percent "yes." King refused to pass conscription and began a campaign to recruit volunteers for overseas service.

▌ In total, William Lyon Mackenzie King served as prime minister of Canada for almost 22 years.

In 1944, the battle for Europe had begun, and the losses were high. Facing protest in Parliament and a Cabinet revolt, King invoked conscription. Approximately 13,000 men were sent overseas for duty. Since King had tried his utmost to avoid conscription, French Canadians were understanding, and the country was not torn apart.

Savings and Rations

In 1942, Canadians received ration books to limit their purchases of goods that were needed for the war effort. Weekly rations of food included 38 grams of tea, 151 grams of coffee, 0.23 kilograms of sugar, and 0.23 kilograms of butter. Ration books and coupons were also provided for gas. To save fabric and buttons for military uniforms, the government set limits on the amount of material that could be used as frills, cuffs, hems, and ruffles on clothing. Dresses were limited to nine buttons.

The steel that had once made washing machines now made bombers. After 1942, no new cars were manufactured in Canada until the war's conclusion. Five-cent coins were made of zinc so nickel could be used in the production of tanks. Families donated aluminum cookware to the aircraft industry.

▌ Propaganda posters advised Canadians to save money wherever and whenever possible.

The War Comes To An End

The bombing of Pearl Harbor was a turning point in the war, as it brought the United States into battle. As a result, the Allies began to gain lost ground. Between 1942 and 1943, British and American troops defeated the German and Italian forces in North Africa and invaded Sicily and Italy.

Trying to get control of the eastern front, Hitler decided to invade Russia. Hitler, however, underestimated the Russian forces. The Battle of Stalingrad in the winter of 1942–1943 saw Russia defeat Germany. During the battle, the Russians took 90,000 prisoners, and the German army began to retreat towards Berlin. By mid-1943, u-boats were being destroyed by sonar equipment and shore-based Allied aircraft.

On June 4, 1944, the Allied armies entered Rome. Six days later, D-Day took place on the shores of Normandy. Americans and **Free French** forces liberated Paris in August. It took 11 months before western troops met their Soviet Allies near the Elbe River in central Germany. Canadians were given the task of clearing German forces from the French, Belgian, and Dutch ports.

■ The Battle of Stalingrad is often referred to as the German army's greatest defeat. It was also one of the most brutal battles of World War II.

■ Hitler decided to override his non-aggression pact with the Soviet Union in 1941. His plan to invade the Soviet Union was called Operation Barbarossa.

On April 27, 1945, Italy's leader, Benito Mussolini, was captured and shot by his own people. Three days later in his underground bunker, Hitler took his own life. On May 8, 1945, Germany surrendered unconditionally. This was V-E, or Victory in Europe, Day.

Meanwhile, the American navy had all but destroyed the Japanese navy and air force, and Commonwealth forces were pushing the Japanese out of Burma, India, and New Guinea. On August 6, 1945, the *Enola Gay*, an American bomber, flew high over the Japanese city of Hiroshima. The plane dropped a single bomb, nicknamed "Little Boy." For the first time in history, an atomic bomb was unleashed on the world. It is estimated that about 140,000 people died as a result of the bombing, many of them suffering slow, painful deaths from radiation poisoning. Following the attack, the United States demanded that the Japanese surrender. There was no reply. Three days later, the bombing was repeated at Nagasaki. Eighty-thousand more people were incinerated in a nuclear inferno. Japan surrendered unconditionally on August 15, 1945, or V-J Day. World War II was over.

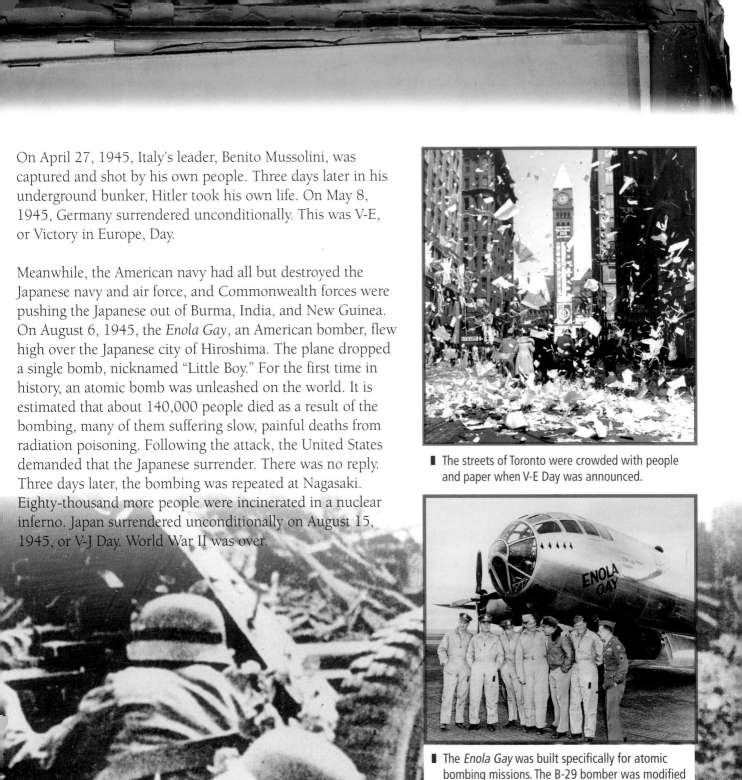

▐ The streets of Toronto were crowded with people and paper when V-E Day was announced.

▐ The *Enola Gay* was built specifically for atomic bombing missions. The B-29 bomber was modified to handle the special requirements of carrying an atomic bomb.

World War II brought many changes to Canada. With the return to peacetime, many people married and had children. The country experienced a baby boom that lasted into the 1960s. Immigration policies relaxed, allowing many people to move to Canada. The country's cultural diversity expanded as a result. The economy grew, and the country recovered from the restrictions and losses the war had brought.

VETERANS AFFAIRS

When soldiers began arriving back in Canada, it became apparent to the government that many of them would require special services. Many had suffered serious injuries, including the loss of limbs and eyesight. Others suffered psychological conditions that needed intensive treatment. Even those soldiers who came home healthy needed to re-adjust to civilian life, find jobs, and earn a living.

In response to these needs, the government created the Department of Veterans Affairs to provide veterans of the war with medical treatment, rehabilitation, education, insurance, welfare, and housing. Many veterans received grants to become farmers and commercial fishermen. About 50,000 veterans received free university tuition. Carleton University in Ottawa was created mainly to educate veterans.

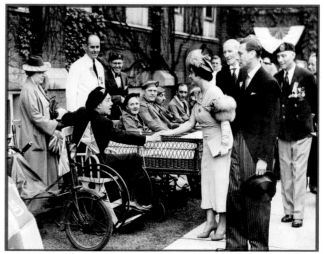

▮ War wounded from both world wars often stayed in veterans' hospitals while they recovered from their injuries. In 1939, King George VI and Queen Elizabeth visited the Christie Veterans' Hospital in Toronto.

WAR BRIDES

Most of the Canadian soldiers who went overseas for war were not married. While in Europe, many of them met and married European women. After the war, the Canadian population exploded as a result. In 1946, 45,000 European "war brides" and their 22,000 children came to Canada with their Canadian husbands.

The Canadian government provided these women and children with sea and rail transport so they could travel to Canada. They were given food allowances and medical care on the boats and trains.

Most war brides were British. In fact, the Canadians were so popular with English women that the Canadian Wives' Bureau was set up in London to offer advice about life in Canada. Even so, many war brides were not ready for the differences between Europe and Canada. They had to adjust to a new way of life.

▮ Transporting war brides to Canada took years. The final shipload of war brides arrived in Canada in 1948.

THE BABY BOOM

The end of the war was a time for celebration and enjoying life. While some soldiers brought European wives home, others came back and married Canadian women. For most of these young couples, the end of the war meant that it was time to start a family. In short time, the "baby boom" commenced. Lasting until 1965, the boom saw a more than 18 percent increase in the birth rate in Canada alone. Other countries also experienced this wave of births.

To assist families with the additional costs of raising children, the federal government began a family allowance program, which included a "baby bonus" to every family. The money was intended to help families pay for medical and dental expenses, food, and housing for children under 16 years of age. It applied to all families in the country. Family allowances began in 1945 to help families buy goods and services and prevent the type of **recession** that took place after World War I.

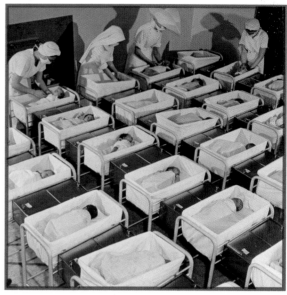

▌ More than 475,000 Canadian babies were born in 1960 alone.

IMMIGRATION AND THE NEED FOR WORKERS

Following World War I, Canada tightened its immigration laws, placing restrictions on who could move to the country. Many of these restrictions indicated racial and ethnic biases, with people from some countries accepted more readily than people from others. These biases continued following World War II.

In 1947, however, the government began reworking its immigration policy. The reasons for these changes were twofold. Canada was a growing economy, and it needed workers. Europe had a number of people who had been displaced as a result of the war. Their homes had been destroyed, and they had no place to live.

The situation was seen as mutually beneficial. People who may not have been accepted into Canada before were now brought in to work on farms, in mines, in the construction industry, or as domestic servants. Most of these immigrants had to commit to working two years in these jobs. Some of the first immigrants to arrive under these new rules were from Poland, Serbia, and Croatia.

▌ Immigrant workers often came to Canada with their families. The influx of people of different cultural backgrounds helped to build Canada's reputation as a multicultural country.

By The Numbers

Gender in the Military

Of the more than one million Canadians that enlisted for World War II, most were men. This chart shows the ratio between men and women.

Women 4%

Men 96%

Source: Veterans Canada

Enlistment by Province

People from all over the country enlisted in the Canadian armed forces. This chart indicates the percentage of enlistees that came from each province.

Province	%	Province	%
Prince Edward Island	1%	Manitoba	7%
Nova Scotia	6%	Saskatchewan	8%
New Brunswick	4%	Alberta	8%
Quebec	17%	British Columbia	9%
Ontario	39%	Unstated	1%

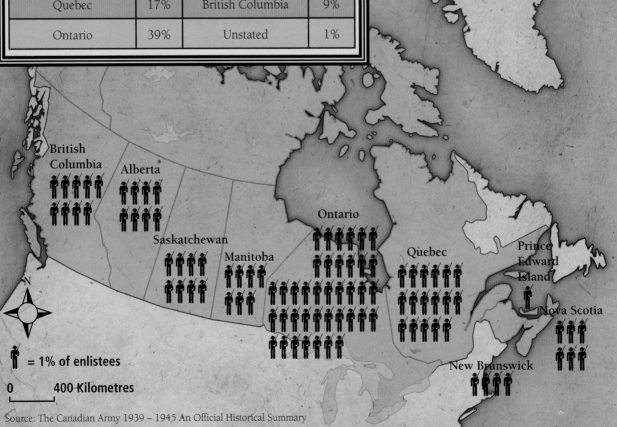

British Columbia

Alberta

Saskatchewan

Manitoba

Ontario

Quebec

Prince Edward Island

Nova Scotia

New Brunswick

N

= 1% of enlistees

0   400 Kilometres

Source: The Canadian Army 1939 – 1945 An Official Historical Summary

Canadian Casualties in World War II

More than 45,000 Canadian military personnel lost their lives in World War II. Many more were wounded. This chart indicates the distribution between fatal and non-fatal casualties.

Fatal Casualties 45%

Non-Fatal Casualties 55%

Source: Veterans Canada

The Cost of War

This chart shows the funds the Canadian government allotted to the war effort for each year. Even though the war ended in 1945, war spending continued as soldiers and families had to be brought to Canada. Government departments had to be restructured as well.

Canadian Government War Expenditure

Year	War Spending	Year	War Spending
1939-1940	$118,291,021.64	1945-1946	$4,002,949,197.25
1940-1941	$752,045,326.06	1946-1947	$1,314,798,107.16
1941-1942	$1,339,674,152.42	1947-1948	$634,421,025.59
1942-1943	$3,724,248,890.27	1948-1949	$425,573,782.37
1943-1944	$4,587,023,093.85	1949-1950	$468,606,607.30
1944-1945	$4,418,446,315.21		

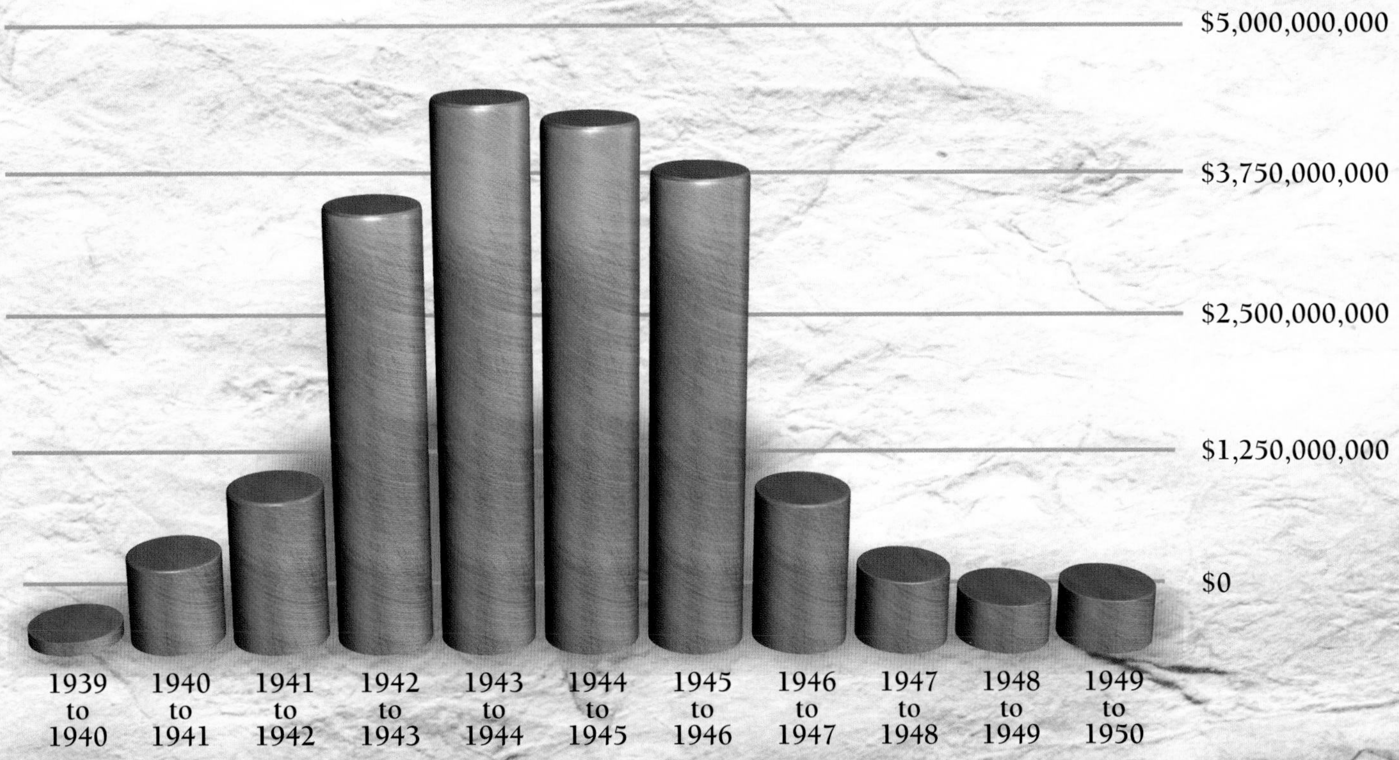

$5,000,000,000

$3,750,000,000

$2,500,000,000

$1,250,000,000

$0

| 1939 to 1940 | 1940 to 1941 | 1941 to 1942 | 1942 to 1943 | 1943 to 1944 | 1944 to 1945 | 1945 to 1946 | 1946 to 1947 | 1947 to 1948 | 1948 to 1949 | 1949 to 1950 |

Estimating war dead is difficult. War causes mass movements of people, many fleeing at short notice. Some move from one country to another. Others move across the globe to another continent. Many never return to their homeland. This movement makes it hard for countries to track their citizens. Death toll estimates for World War II range from 50 million to 70 million people. Many of these people died in military service for their country. Others were civilians who were killed as a result of the action happening around them. It is estimated that about six million Jews died during the **Holocaust**.

This chart shows some of the countries that experienced major losses during the war.

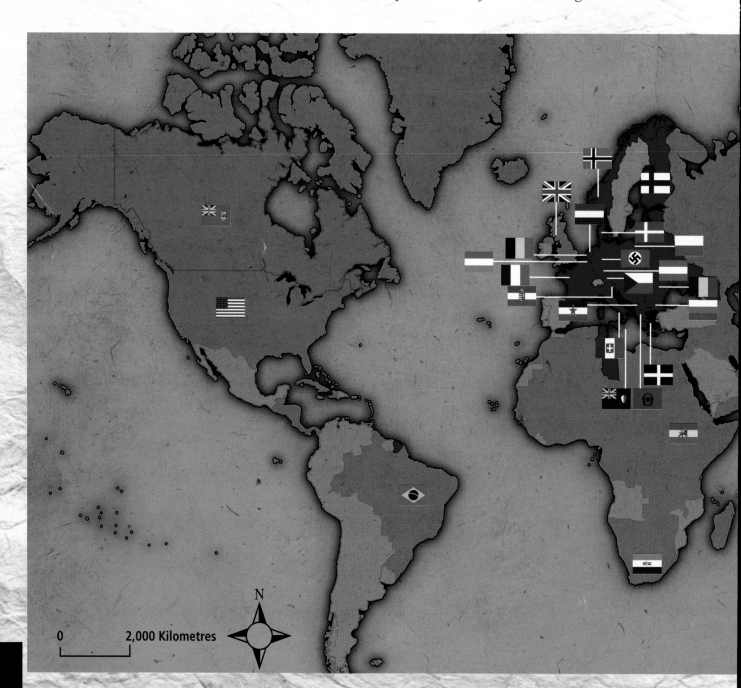

0   2,000 Kilometres

N

ALLIED POWERS

Country	Military Deaths	Civilian Deaths	Total Deaths
Soviet Union	10,000,000	10,000,000	20,000,000
China	2,500,000	7,500,00	10,000,000
United States	400,000	0	400,000
United Kingdom	326,000	62,000	388,000
Canada	45,300	0	45,300
India	24,000	13,000	37,000
Australia	23,000	12,000	35,000
New Zealand	10,000	2,000	12,000
South Africa	7,000	0	7,000
Ethiopia	5,000	0	5,000
Brazil	1,000	0	1,000
Malta	0	2,000	2,000
Allied Total	**13,341,300**	**17,591,000**	**30,932,300**

AXIS POWERS and OCCUPIED AREAS

Country	Military Deaths	Civilian Deaths	Total Deaths
Germany	3,500,000	700,000	4,200,000
Japan	2,000,000	350,000	2,350,000
Romania	300,000	160,000	460,000
Hungary	140,000	290,000	430,000
Italy	330,000	80,000	410,000
Austria	230,000	104,000	334,000
Finland	82,000	2,000	84,000
Poland	100,000	5,700,000	5,800,000
Yugoslavia	300,000	1,400,000	1,700,000
France	250,000	350,000	600,000
Czechoslovakia	200,000	215,000	415,000
Netherlands	12,000	198,000	210,000
Greece	20,000	140,000	160,000
Belgium	12,000	76,000	88,000
Albania	28,000	2,000	30,000
Bulgaria	10,000	10,000	20,000
Norway	6,400	3,900	10,300
Luxembourg	5,000	0	5,000
Denmark	400	1,000	1,400
Axis Total	**7,525,800**	**9,781,900**	**17,307,700**

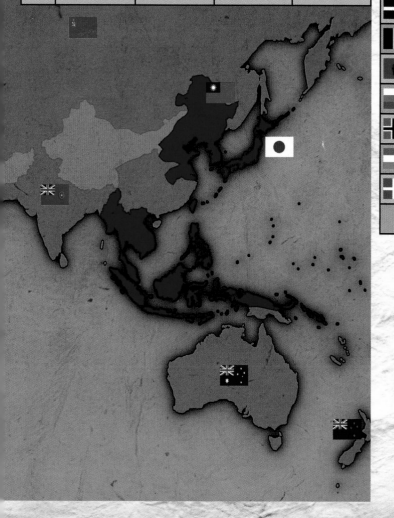

How We Remember

More than 42,000 men and women of Canada's armed forces died during the war, while approximately 54,000 others were wounded. Another 9,000 were taken prisoner. There are currently more than 6,000 war memorials in Canada paying tribute to these individuals. Some memorials commemorate specific battles or campaigns. Others honour the fallen or those without a tombstone.

Camp X Memorial, Intrepid Park, Ontario

Today, all that remains of Camp X is a park commemorating where the camp once stood. The Camp X Memorial sits inside the park, overlooking the waters of Lake Ontario. It honours the men and women who trained at Camp X.

National War Memorial, Ottawa, Ontario

The National War Memorial in Ottawa was originally constructed to remember those who died in World War I. However, when World War II ended, the dates of that war were added to one side of the monument. Today, the monument stands as a memorial to all Canadians who have died in war.

First Flight, Winnipeg, Manitoba

The First Flight memorial stands on the grounds of Manitoba's legislature. It is a statue of a World War II airman. The memorial is dedicated to all of the instructors and trainees who died in Canada while training in the Commonwealth Air Training Plan.

Canadians are also remembered in other parts of the world. Memorials have been built all over the world to pay tribute to these people and the efforts they made on behalf of peace and freedom. Special tributes are paid to these brave men and women on days of remembrance.

Juno Beach Centre, France

The Juno Beach Centre serves as a memorial as well as an interactive educational facility and museum. It offers information about Canada's role in World War II. The centre was built on the site where Canadian troops landed on D-Day.

Sai Wan Memorial, Hong Kong

The Sai Wan Memorial pays tribute to the Commonwealth soldiers who lost their lives during the Battle of Hong Kong. The memorial stands at the entrance to the war cemetery. The names of the more than 2,000 soldiers, including the 228 Canadians, who died in the battle are inscribed on the monument's walls.

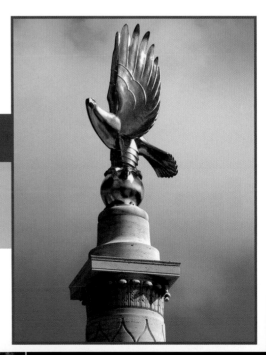

Malta Memorial, Malta

The Malta Memorial is dedicated to the almost 2,300 Commonwealth airmen who served in Malta in World War II. The memorial consists of a marble column with a bronze eagle at the top. The names of 285 Canadian airmen are among those engraved on the memorial.

Timeline

The War Overseas

May 10, 1940
Germany invades Belgium, Holland, and Luxembourg.

December 7–8, 1941
The Japanese attack Pearl Harbor and Hong Kong.

September 1, 1939
Germany invades Poland.

June 22, 1941
Germany invades the Soviet Union.

August 19, 1942
The raid on Dieppe takes place.

September 3, 1939
Great Britain and France declare war on Germany.

1939 **1941**

1940 **1942**

The War at Home

September 10, 1939
Canada declares war on Germany.

1941
Wage and price controls begin in Canada.

August 17, 1943–June 4, 1944
The Allies, including Canadian forces, invade and capture Sicily and Italy.

August 6 and 9, 1945
Atomic bombs are dropped on Hiroshima and Nagasaki.

June 6, 1944
Canadians land on Juno Beach in France and take part in D-Day.

May 8, 1945
V-E Day is declared to celebrate the Allied victory in Europe.

August 15, 1945
V-J Day is declared to celebrate victory over the Japanese. World War II ends.

1943 **1944** **1945**

April 1942
Canada holds a plebiscite on conscription. The government decides to conscript soldiers for duty only within Canada.

November 1944
Canada conscripts 13,000 troops for overseas duty.

Test Yourself

Multiple Choice

1. What country did Germany invade to cause Great Britain and France to declare war?
   a. Czechoslovakia
   b. Poland
   c. Austria
   d. Ethiopia

2. Which two countries signed the Non-Aggression Pact in August 1939?
   a. Germany and France
   b. France and Great Britain
   c. Germany and the Soviet Union
   d. Soviet Union and Great Britain

3. Where did the first Canadian military engagement of the war take place?
   a. Hong Kong
   b. France
   c. Stalingrad
   d. Sicily

4. What was Germany's goal in fighting the Battle of the Atlantic?
   a. to destroy the United States Navy
   b. to stop supplies from getting to Great Britain
   c. to secure the eastern front
   d. to destroy British munitions factories

5. Which Canadian developed a system for degaussing ships?
   a. Tommy Prince
   b. George Klein
   c. William Henderson
   d. Charles Goodeve

6. Which of the following tanks was built in Canada?
   a. Sherman
   b. Valentine
   c. Lee-Enfield
   d. Leopard

7. Why were Japanese Canadians sent to internment camps?
   a. the attack on Pearl Harbor
   b. the Battle of Hong Kong
   c. Japanese aggression in Asia
   d. all of the above

8. What was the task of the RCN during the war?
   a. to provide protection for the supply convoys
   b. to destroy German U-boats
   c. none of the above
   d. all of the above

9. When were women permitted to join the army?
   a. 1939
   b. 1940
   c. 1941
   d. 1943

True or False

1. The army was the first division of Canada's armed forces to accept women.

2. Camp X was used to train Allied pilots.

3. Enigma was a special code used by the Germans.

4. ASDIC is a type of radar.

5. D-Day is also known as Operation Overlord.

6. World War II brought an end to the Great Depression.

7. Most war brides came from France.

8. The baby boom lasted until 1965.

Mix 'n Match

1. William Lyon Mackenzie King

2. The Axis

3. D-Day

4. Pearl Harbor

5. Benito Mussolini

6. Camp X

7. Joseph Stalin

a. spy training centre near Oshawa, Ontario
b. prime minister of Canada
c. leader of Italy
d. alliance led by Germany
e. Allied invasion of France
f. leader of the Soviet Union
g. American naval base in Hawaii

Canada's Role in the War

Only 20 years separated World War I and World War II. Yet, in that time, Canada had experienced much change. These changes had an impact on how Canada participated in the war.

Using books and the Internet, compare Canada's role in World War I and World War II. Pay close attention to the political, economical, and social conditions in Canada at the time, as well as the country's technological capabilities during each war. Then, answer the following questions.

- How did these differences affect Canada's role in each war?

- How did Canada's contributions in each war affect Canada's international reputation?

- How did Canada grow as a country following each war?

Glossary

artillery: large guns used by an army or the troops that use them

Austro-Hungarian Empire: the dual monarchy established in 1867, consisting of what are now Austria, Hungary, the Czech Republic, Slovakia, Slovenia, Croatia, and Bosnia-Herzegovina, and parts of Poland, Romania, Ukraine, and Italy

battalion: a military unit made up of a headquarters and two or more companies

batteries: army artillery units

Battle of Britain: a series of intense raids directed against Great Britain by the German air force in World War II

chancellor: a country's head of government

civilian: a person who is not a member of the military

colonial: relating to colonies, or areas that remain under the control of another country

conscription: required enrolment in military service

convoys: vehicles travelling together with a protective escort

corvettes: fast, lightly armed warships

D-Day: the day that the Allied forces invaded France during World War II

decorated: awarded medals for bravery or service

encrypted: using a secret code

fission: the splitting of an atomic nucleus into approximately equal parts

Free French: a French movement during World War II that was organized to fight for the liberation of France from Germany

fusion: the process by which nuclear reactions between light elements form a heavier one, releasing huge amounts of energy

garrison duty: assigned to protect a fortified place

Great Depression: a severe worldwide economic slowdown in the decade preceding World War II

heavy water: water enriched in deuterium, an isotope of hydrogen

Holocaust: the systematic killing of Jews by the Nazi regime before and during World War II

Imperial Conference of 1937: a meeting held by members of the British Commonwealth to discuss mutual issues

infantry: an army unit consisting of soldiers who fight on foot

infiltration: the process of secretly gaining access to enemy territory

intelligence: military information about enemies and spies

internment: confinement during wartime

multilateralism: countries working together on an issue

Nuremberg Laws: laws the Nazi Party put into effect in 1935 to strip Germany's Jews of their German citizenship and the rights that accompany it

occupied: an area that has been invaded by the enemy

paratroopers: soldiers trained in parachuting

photo cells: cells that, when exposed to light, generate an electric current

pillboxes: a low-roofed concrete structure in which a machine gun or antitank gun sits

platoon: a subdivision of a company of troops

propaganda: information, ideas, or rumours deliberately spread to help or harm a person, group, or nation

recession: a period of economic decline

reconnaissance missions: exploratory surveys of an area

referendum: a vote by which people directly decide between two or more choices on a major issue

resistance group: an underground organization trying to liberate a country under military occupation

right-wing government: a government that supports the preservation of social order or traditional values

status: a federally registered member of a First Nation, having special privileges under the law

theatres of war: the entire land, sea, and air area directly involved in war operations

Index